I0141122

Too Blessed and Highly Favored To be Stressed

Rebecca Simmons

Diligence Publishing Company
Bloomfield, New Jersey

The Scripture in this book is from the King James Version, New Living Translation, and the New International Version with some verses paraphrased.

Book cover assistance by Nuvision Designs

Copyright © 2025 Rebecca Simmons
c/o Diligence Publishing Company
P.O. Box 2476
Bloomfield, New Jersey

All Rights Reserved

No part of this book may be reproduced in any form without the written permission from the publisher except for brief passages included in a review.

To contact Rebecca Simmons to preach or speak at your church, organization, seminar, or conference email:

ISBN: 979-8-9869173-6-8

Printed in the United States

TABLE OF CONTENTS

DEDICATION

This book is dedicated to my mother, who will always tell you that she is blessed and highly favored of the Lord, to my husband, my sisters and brothers, my children, my church family, and all of my spiritual children and those connected to me through NCCM, WDFV, and MKGN – thank you for your love, commitment, and prayers.

This book is also dedicated to everyone who has ever felt forsaken, forgotten, stressed out, or overwhelmed. May this book remind you that God never overlooks what He has ordained and that you truly are too blessed and highly favored to be stressed.

CHAPTER 1

LET US PRAY

I'm glad you're reading this book. God has some things He wants to say to you as you read these pages. I challenge you to read this book to the end. I know you're ready to dive in so let us begin. I want to open this book with prayer. Let us pray:

Father God, we praise your holy name. We give you the glory, the honor, and the praise. We magnify your name; we exalt your name. Lord, we glorify your name. We thank you for this day. This is the day that you have made, and we are rejoicing and being glad in it, in spite of the storms of life, in spite of the trials, in spite of the tribulation, in spite of what we may be facing. Lord, we come before you. We come with the spirit of exaltation. We come with the spirit of praise. We praise you today and always, Lord.

We declare and decree that no weapon formed against us can prosper. We are the head, we are the top, we are the healed, Oh God. We are the delivered. We are the victorious. We are the sons and daughters of God, of the Most High. We are blessed, and highly favored, and we thank you for blessing us, Lord. We praise you.

Thank you for the person who is reading this prayer right now. We are on individual journeys, but we know that everyone goes through tough times in life, and there comes a time when we need you more than ever. So have your way Lord. Have your way even as I share what you have given me to share in this book. Let your will be done. Let your will be done on earth as you have already ordained in Heaven. Let your Spirit move, God. Let your Spirit speak, Oh God. In the name of Jesus.

Lord, we thank you and we praise you. Touch that woman or that man who needs a touch from you now. They don't have to wait until the end of the book or to read and find out how to reject stress and other damaging emotions so they can continually manifest being too blessed to be stressed in every area of their life. Touch them now.

Touch that woman that needs a reminder of who you say she is. Touch that man that needs a reminder of his Kingdom identity. Touch that one that's been, oh, God, my God, wrestling with you. Oh, God, that one who says, Lord, I'm not going to let you go until you bless me, Lord, touch her.

Touch him. Touch the one that's discouraged, the one that may be feeling a little bit frustrated. Lord, touch that one who is feeling a little bit lonely, touch them. Lord, touch. Touch that one who has been afflicted with sickness in mind, body, emotions, or spirit. They need a touch from you Lord. Touch them now.

And that one who's feeling empowered, oh God, touch that one Lord and fill them with even more of your anointing. Touch that one who feels like they can soar right now and lift them even higher. Touch the one who's on the verge of breakthrough and bring them all the way out! Bring them all the way into their place of victory! Touch Lord in the name of Jesus!

Lord, we thank you. We praise you. We glorify your name. Thank you for your presence even as we continue in the pages of this book. We thank you for your presence as each page is read. Have your way. Let your will be done. In Jesus' name we pray, Amen.

Surely, Lord, you bless the righteous; you surround them with your favor as with a shield.

Psalm 5:12
New International Version

CHAPTER 2

DON'T LET IT MAKE YOU CHANGE YOUR NAME

The Scripture that I'm using as the basis for the message in this book comes from the book of Ruth, Chapter 1. As I was reading the Scripture in those verses, this was in my spirit: Too blessed to be stressed. I'm blessed. I am too blessed to be stressed. I preached a message about it to my mentees in Women Destined For Victory. They were really blessed by it, so I decided to write this book to share with you and let you know that no matter what, and in spite of anything that you are going through in life, you really are too blessed to be stressed. It is my goal to have you reject stress and any negative emotions and get it deep down in your spirit as you begin to declare out of your own mouth that not only are you too blessed to be stressed, but you are too blessed and highly favored to be stressed!

Let's take a look at the Scripture:

Ruth Chapter One verses 12-21 (This is Ruth talking to her daughters-in-law):

Turn again my daughters go your way; for I am too old to have a husband. If I should say I have hope. If I should have a husband also tonight and should also bear sons; would you wait for them until they are grown? Would you stay for them from having husbands? No my daughters, for it grieves me much for your sakes, that the hand of the LORD has gone out against me.

And they lifted up their voice, and wept again. And Orpah kissed her mother-in-law, but Ruth held tightly to her.

And she said, Behold, thy sister-in-law is gone back to her people, and to her gods; return thou after thy sister-in-law, And Ruth said, intreat me not to leave thee, or to return from following after thee. But where you go, I will go, and where you lodge I will lodge. Your people shall be my people, and your God my God. Where you die, I will die, and there will I be buried, and the Lord do so to me and more if anything but death come between you and me. When she saw that she was steadfastly minded to go with her, then she left speaking unto her, (she stopped trying to convince her to leave her).

So they too went until they came to Bethlehem. And it came to pass when they were come to

Bethlehem, that all the city was moved about them. And they said, Is this Naomi?

And she said unto them, Call me not Naomi, call me Mara: for the Almighty has dealt very bitterly with me. I went out full and the LORD has brought me home again empty. Why then call me Naomi, seeing the Lord has testified against me, and the Almighty has afflicted me?

As we read these verses, there is a double-edged theme shouting back at us. One is, "Don't let it change your name. Don't let the circumstances, the situations, other people's opinions, the struggle, or life, change your name. Don't let it change your name.

It can also be worded as "Don't let it make you change your name." This fits even better because the circumstances that Naomi was facing in life did not change Naomi's name. Naomi allowed what she was going through to make her change her name.

In the Hebrew language, Naomi's name means pleasant, gentle. It also means pleasantness or delight. In essence, when the people were asking, "Is this Naomi?" she was responding, "Don't call me pleasant, don't call me delight, don't call me that. Call me Mara." Mara means bitter. She said, "Call me Mara."

She was saying, I'm bitter. I don't feel pleasant. I'm not feeling good about life. I'm not feeling good about myself and my circumstances. Just call me Mara because the LORD has dealt bitterly with me. God has dealt me a bitter blow.

Naomi was. feeling some kind of way about life. She was feeling some kind of way about God, and it was not good.

That was the first thing that I was thinking. "Don't let it change your name" or "Don't let it make you change your name." You could take it either way. And then the other thing that this particular Scripture text prompted me to do was to remind you that you are too blessed and highly favored to be stressed. As Kingdom citizens and children of the Most High God, we are too blessed to be stressed. One of the names God calls you is "Blessed." And we know that whatever God has spoken has and will come to pass. Whom God has blessed is blessed. Don't let life, pain, anger, frustration, or bitterness make you change your name. You are "Blessed."

Because of who you are in Christ, you have received favor. God's favor is on your life.

In Luke 1:28 The angel came to Mary and said, *"Greetings, you who are highly favored. The Lord is with you. Blessed are you among women."*

Why was Mary considered to be highly favored and blessed among women? Mary was chosen.

She was handpicked by God for a special assignment. Her assignment was greater than any assignment – before or after – given to a woman or any person other than Jesus Christ. Mary was chosen to carry Jesus in her womb. She was chosen to be the virgin that gave birth to our LORD and Savior!

Although we can never be as blessed and highly favored as Mary, the mother of Jesus, we can rejoice in the fact that God has chosen us and set us apart to advance His Kingdom in the earth realm. We are all here on assignment, a peculiar people, a royal priesthood, chosen – handpicked by God for such a time as this!

Just like Mary was on assignment, whether Naomi knew it or not, she was on assignment and she was blessed and highly favored.

You also need to know that in spite of your circumstances, you also are here in the earth realm on divine assignment. You have a mandate, a mantle, a mountain, and a metron (measure) that has been assigned specifically to you by God even while you were still in your mother's womb.

Pray and get clarity on your assignment, ask for wisdom and the blueprint to carry it out, Study to get the knowledge you need, practice to be skillful in your Kingdom task, and stand in the power of God's might against the adversary, the battles, and the issues of life that will come to make you throw up your hands and give up. Never give up, and do not ever allow the battle to frustrate you or make you bitter. Stand firm in your identity as one who has been chosen and set apart for Kingdom purpose. Whatever happens, know that God is working in the middle of it for your good. Whatever happens, do not let it make you change your name.

CHAPTER 3

HATERS ARE ALWAYS HATING

Let's step back and look at the context of the text from the book of Ruth. Naomi's husband and her only two sons had died in Moab. She was in the grip of grief. We never want to make grief or losing a loved one a small thing. Naomi had every right to be stressed out. She had every right to be angry.

There are things that you can go through in life that bring turbulence to you and that can bring pain to your heart and bitterness to your soul. I was thinking recently about Hannah and Peninnah. We know the story of Hannah and Peninnah. Their story can be found in 1 Samuel, Chapter 1 in the Bible. They were both married to a man named Elkanah. Hannah did not have any children. She was barren. But Peninnah had children, and Peninnah began to vex Hannah. She began to grievously taunt Hannah. I can imagine her saying, "Aha, Aha. You don't have no children. Aha, Aha. Precious Hannah can't produce. Hannah banana is barren! I'm blessed. I'm more blessed than you because I have given Elkanah children and you can't."

Sometimes it's crazy. I said this when I was teaching about this in Bible study one Wednesday. It's crazy how sometimes people can be more blessed than you. They can be seemingly more favored than you and still hate on and be jealous of you. It could seem like life is going perfectly for them and you're struggling and going through all kinds of changes, all kinds of frustration, all kinds of bitterness, all kinds of trials and tribulations. But they still want to hate on and be jealous of you!

That lets us know that things are not always what they seem. There are still a lot of dysfunctional people out there wearing masks of perfection and picking on you. There is a saying that misery loves company, and it's true. If their lives were so perfect, they would not be hating on you. Let that sink in.

The truth of the matter is there will always be someone out there looking at you and disliking you, being jealous of you, talking negatively about you, and shooting word daggers at you. There are a lot of undercover and overt haters out there, and until the Lord delivers them, haters are going to keep doing what they do – hating!

Peninnah was jealous of Hannah because Elkanah loved Hannah more. He favored her more and he blessed her with more than he blessed everyone else with. Although Hannah was barren and hated by her adversary, she was still blessed. I feel like shouting right here. Although you may not be producing like you think you should. Although other people may be producing more than you or look more blessed than you, know this – you are still blessed, and you are still favored! Let the haters hate, because having haters is a sign that your time of manifestation is coming.

David wrote this declaration in the Bible in Psalm 23:

You prepare a table before me in the presence of my enemies; you anoint my head with oil; my cup overflows.

Make that declaration over your own life and watch God set the table and overflow your cup!

Don't worry about the haters. God has not forgotten you! Even in the middle of warfare, God is preparing a table of blessings in the face of your enemies. God is preparing to bless you right in front of those who mock you, count you out, spread rumors about you, or who just don't like you for whatever reason they may have. Keep

19

walking with God. Not only is the table being prepared, but there is an anointing that comes from the battle. There is an anointing that comes from the pressure of being laughed at, rejected, and seemingly barren. Power is produced in the press. Character is produced in the press. Weightier anointing is produced in the press. A closer walk with God is produced in the press. Obedience is produced in the press, overflow is produced in the press, and finally, fresh oil is produced in the press. You get even more oily under pressure. The oil of the press makes you oily. It gives you the anointing for great exploits and victory.

Do not worry. Do not fear. Do not be dismayed by the haters. Make the declaration from Psalm 23 over your own life and watch God set the table and overflow your cup! Blessings, anointing, and overflow are coming your way. So let them hate. Haters are always hating, but God is always working on your behalf for your good. God has a plan, and His plan is to prosper you and not to harm you, to give you a hope and a future. Let them hate, but you be sure to continue to give God praise!

CHAPTER 4

GOD IS WAITING ON YOU

Listen. Everybody is dealing with something in life. Nobody has a perfect life. We all have our own cross to bear, The apostle Paul said there was a thorn given to him – a thorn in the flesh, a messenger of Satan to buffet him. He said he asked God three times to take the thorn away from him. And God told him, "My grace is sufficient for you. My power is made great in your weakness. (2 Corinthians 12:9)

As I use my spiritual imagination, I interpret God saying, Paul, my grace is sufficient for you. You are too blessed to be stressed because you have my grace. You have my power available to you during this time of weakness.

The definition of this word "grace" is unmerited favor, divine power, enablement, or influence, anointing, and benevolent kindness, which is freely given and available to believers when they need it, especially in times of weakness.

As you can see from the definition above "grace" is not only God's favor and kindness. Grace is also divine power enablement, or influence. I believe God was saying to Paul, my power, my divine influence, my grace which enables you to do all things through me, is sufficient for and available to you. I've given you the ability, I've given you the anointing to walk through this trial and even to have peace in the middle of it. You can handle this thorn in your flesh, Paul. I've given you the power, the ability to overcome it. My ability – My divine Influence – that I've given you is sufficient. My power that is working for, in, and through you is enough.

Sometimes we're asking God to take from us what we can handle. Sometimes we're asking God to do for us what we can do. And God turns that right back around, saying no, you do something, you handle it, you have the ability to do something, and I am backing you up. I am with you. My anointing, my power is with you. It's in you, and when you move in faith, my Spirit will come upon you and equip you to be triumphant.

There are times when we are waiting for God to move, and God is, in fact, waiting for us to move. That's what Naomi did. She was not happy where she was, so she busted a move. She got up and she did something. Sometimes in life when you're not happy with what you are getting, when you are not happy with where you are, you have to do something different or do something differently. You have to shift your position. You just need to move. You may need to do something different, go somewhere different or change the way that you are doing life. You will get an alert through a life storm that says, "danger ahead. It's time to get to a place of safety. It's time to change your direction. It's time to get back to prayer. It's time to get back to the house of God. It's time to move from being amongst people who do not align with your faith in God and your mandate. It's time to move and get back to being around people of great faith. It's time to shift your position and get to the place where God has prepared for you to receive what you need to receive in order to manifest your next season, assignment, and or blessing.

That's what Naomi did. Chances are she said to herself, I'm getting up out of here. Moab is not being good to me.

Technically speaking, being an Israelite, she was not even supposed to be in Moab. Moab was where the enemies of Israel were. Moab was where the enemies of God dwelt. The Moabites often opposed the Israelites and were condemned for their pride and idol worship. Naomi's husband had relocated his family there during the famine in Bethlehem Judah in search of food and a better life. He was doing the right thing in trying to provide for and make a better life for his family, but he was in the wrong place!

Sometimes you can be in the wrong place, around the wrong people, trying to do the right thing, and the Spirit of God will let you know that you have to get up out of there. I remember being in our old church, which was a very good ministry, and God began to call my husband and I out to plant and pastor a church. We did not want to go. We had gotten saved in that church and were members for over 11 years. We were serving in various ministries, and we liked where we were. But God had another plan. I'll never forget when God started calling us out. We were moving real slow in obeying Him. Then one night, we were watching a preacher on television, and the preacher said these words, "If you are in the wrong place, doing the right thing, you are ineffective for the Kingdom of God."

I literally fell off the couch onto the floor with tears in my eyes. That was the day, I gave God another yes. We put our hands to the plow. It's been over 20 years, and we have not looked back. Although the dynamics and functions have changed, my husband and I are still doing the work of the ministry that God has called us to do. Over the years, we have learned that we must obey God. Obedience is key. When you move in obedience to the voice and will of God, God moves to bless you in that area.

My experience and talking to many who have come to a place where they no longer feel connected to the church they are in has taught me that sometimes you can be in the wrong church. Not that it was always the wrong church, or not that there is anything wrong with that church, but it could be that you have come to a place in your spiritual walk where God is shifting you. He may be calling you to another church or to another level of ministry.

God does not always call you out of your church or ministry that you have been in for a long time. Sometimes He calls you up into leadership at that local assembly or within that ministry. Always pray and discern the will of God when it comes to what He is doing as you mature in your walk with Him and feel the prompting of the call to ministry or the prompting to leave a church or ministry. Make sure you are hearing God before you make a move.

I also advise that you sit down and talk to your leaders. Your pastor or spiritual leader is human and has feelings. Chances are they care for you and don't want you to leave. Sit down and have a conversation to communicate what's going on with you. If you have to go, go in peace. Don't burn bridges. God is not pleased when we do that.

You can also find yourself in the wrong romantic relationship, wrong friendships, or connected to the wrong people. Sometimes you could be at the wrong job. Sometimes you could be doing the wrong mandate, in the wrong metron (measure of territory or capacity), or the wrong network. God will shift you, and He will compel you to pivot and reposition yourself. Again, discernment and obeying the Spirit of God is of the utmost importance. Pray and ask God, Lord, what should I do?"

Then search your heart and ask yourself, *What is God saying about this?*

In most cases, the answer is just a prayer or a single thought away.

Sometimes even being fired or being laid off from a job is God shifting and repositioning you. It doesn't feel good. The shift does not always feel good, but it's necessary.

The repositioning did not feel good to Naomi. She lost both sons. She lost her husband. She was grieving. But she was moving. You know, even in the middle of grief, we must find ourselves continuing to keep moving. As you move in the middle of grief or hardship, know that you are never alone. God is right there moving with you. He is guiding you along the way, taking you to a place of healing, taking you to a place of grace,

power, and peace. Will you move with God? He is
waiting on you.

The LORD had said to Abram, "Go from your country, your people and your father's household to the land I will show you. "I will make you into a great nation, and I will bless you; I will make your name great, and you will be a blessing.³I will bless those who bless you, and whoever curses you I will curse; and all peoples on earth will be blessed through you."

So Abram went, as the LORD had told him; and Lot went with him. Abram was seventy-five years old when he set out from Harran.

Genesis 12:1-4 (NIV(

CHAPTER 5

WARFARE BRINGS OUT THE WARRIOR IN YOU

I was having dinner with some people one Saturday, and one of them said that sometimes you could be hurting because of things you have gone through or are going through in life and doing so much that you don't even know you're hurting.

I looked at her and said, "I can't identify with that because when I'm hurting, I know I'm hurting."

I'm so sensitive in the Spirit that I know when the enemy comes to crush my spirit. And that's what spiritual warfare does, it comes to crush your spirit.

I would say that Naomi and Hannah were going through some spiritual warfare. The enemy was using life's circumstances to crush their spirits, but in the end, both of these women proved to be too blessed and highly favored to be stressed. They went through the process of the pain of the spiritual attack, and they both prevailed.

During that conversation at dinner, I thought to myself, *I know when I'm hurting.*

Now, what the person said is true for some people. There are people hurting and bleeding all over the place, and they have covered up their pain for so long that they are numb to the fact that they are actually still hurting. But if you are like me, you know when you are hurting. If you are like me, you have suffered through some stuff. And you felt the pain of that thing, you felt the sting down in your core.

When somebody hurts my feelings or when something hurts me, I feel that thing and my spirit has to fight to keep my flesh from lashing out and retaliating. Can you identify? Can you identify that you have to fight your flesh sometimes and hold yourself back from going off on somebody? Can you identify that you have to fight your flesh sometimes in order not to curse somebody out, not to complain, not to get depressed, not to fall into a rut or go hide in a cave somewhere?

I must confess. I have to fight my flesh at times. I have to fight not to get into the flesh and to stay in the Spirit. People say to me, "Oh, you're so deep. You're so radical. You are so strong," but they don't know the cost. They don't know the old me. I thank God that like Paul, I've learned to beat my flesh into subjection to keep the old me from rising up.

As a kingdom warrior you too must fight to not allow yourself to fight your battles in the flesh. When the old you tries to rise up while God is working on the new you, developing you, shaping you and molding you into the image of His Son, make sure that you don't give in to your emotions.

The old you will at times try to rise up. You know that old version of you – the needy you, the shame-filled you, the you that keeps giving in to the enemy's accusations because the devil is the accuser of the brethren. What about the guilty you who has already been forgiven but you still feel guilty, and you still hold yourself under condemnation? That's when you have to fight the flesh. You have to say no to the desires of the old nature. What about the you that says, "I don't even want to walk in faith right now?"

You have to fight. You have to fight that version of yourself and continue to walk in the newer version of yourself, which is the faith-filled you, the powerful you. The you that's created in the image of God, the anointed you. My God! The you that's on assignment, the you that knows that you deserve better than anything less than God's best. Fight against spiritual warfare and walk in the power of the warrior you that is more than a conqueror! Yes, there is a warrior in you. You have been chosen to fight the battle of the good fight of faith. You have been chosen to be victorious because greater is God on the inside of you than anything you will face in this world. You have been chosen to be a Kingdom warrior. You have been chosen to take territory according to your God-assigned metron and to move in the measure of grace and the territory given for your purpose in the earth realm. Don't cry over the warfare. Warfare is a part of the territory. Keep fighting and let the warfare bring out the warrior in you!

CHAPTER 6

CONQUERING ATTACKS AGAINST YOUR EMOTIONS

Naomi came to a point in the middle of her trial where she had had enough! She probably said to herself, *I'm going back to Bethlehem. I'm going back to the place where my God and my people dwell.*

That's what we have to do. We have to continue to press our way back into the place where God dwells. We have to press our way into the presence of God because as long as we stay in the place of discouragement or in the place of bitterness without going to God in prayer, we are separated from God and open to the enemy's attacks. In the presence of God is the fullness of joy. In the presence of God is healing. In the presence of God is protection, strength, and peace.

Let me share a testimony with you. I wanted to visit my mother in Florida. We didn't have our

Real ID's yet, and I didn't know we could still fly without it but with the proper documentation, so I asked my husband to drive me to Florida. He agreed and we took a road trip to Florida from New Jersey. We had a great time going and a fabulous time spending time with family in Florida. but coming home from Florida, we had a disagreement. I got upset with my husband and that thing tried to cut me to my core.

God is amazing because He has given us the ability to love and to love deeply. At the same time, the devil is crafty because he will take the people that you love the most and try to use them to hurt you the most. The people that you love the most can hurt you the most because what do you care about strangers? What do you care about that person offending you that you barely know? We don't care as much about people that we are not in a close relationship with as we do about those close to us. We don't usually care about what they say about us or what they think about us. But when you have somebody that's really close to you, like a child, a spouse, a parent, or a really good close friend, then that person and what they do or say, and even what happens to them can penetrate.

So back to my testimony. My husband said something that I didn't like. Or maybe it was that I didn't like the tone in which he said it. It was late at night. We were supposed to be sleeping. We were supposed to be in our hotel already because the agreement was to stop midway and get a hotel room.

So here we are and it's very late at night, we're both tired, and our guards are down. And he said something that I didn't like. In response, I said something not so nice, and we both got angry. Now the old me would have kept pushing until we both worked up a heated state of rage which would have ended up in us having a really big argument. The old me could go from zero to one hundred in my temperament quickly. I could go from being calm and speaking softly to being outraged and screaming within minutes. But none of that happened. I thank God for working on me. I thank God for changing me!

God is still working on us all. I thank God He is not finished with me yet! I knew that I had been promoted when I didn't start yelling or add more negative fuel to the disagreement. We checked into a hotel and went to sleep. But my spirit was still troubled. Even as we drove home the next morning, my spirit was troubled, but I was praying. I was pressing into the presence of God the whole time. We drove about 4 1/2 hours, and although my husband had apologized before we went to sleep, and I had accepted his apology, I was still not at peace.

Listen. Words have power, and the way you say what you say can help or hinder the situation. I often say you have to be careful how you talk to people. Be careful how you treat people. Because your words and the way you say them can leave a lasting and sometimes irreversible impact. For instance, if you hammer a nail into a piece of wood and then pull that nail out, you are still going to have a nail mark. It still leaves a hole where the nail was. That nail made a mark, and it's going to take some work to fix the hole that the nail made. But! We are commanded to forgive, even when people leave a nail mark in our hearts. When people leave a negative impact on our hearts with their actions or their words, we're charged to forgive. You're charged with forgiving those who hurt or mistreated you. That was one thing that I did. I forgave. I was saying to myself, *I'm not going to carry this in my heart.*

Then I let it go! Now I had to process it, but the battle was already won the minute I decided to let it go. And guess what? After calming down and thinking about our disagreement, I realized that I was wrong too. I was wrong with the way I approached my husband, and I was wrong for not seeing that he was tired and for not seeing things from his perspective. My lesson in that is that even though my feelings were hurt, there are always two sides to every story, and there is always more than one way to see what's going on in the middle of a disagreement. Once we got home, I had to humble myself and apologize to my husband as well. And I thanked him for driving me to Florida and back which for him was truly a labor of love.

When you are faced with hurt feelings, anger, discouragement, disappointment, or bitterness, you have to process the anger. You have to process the pain. You have to process the disappointment. You have to process discouragement, but you must not let bitterness take root in your heart. You must let it go. You must forgive the person who has hurt you or done you wrong. Forgiving is your way of giving it to God. It's your way of saying, "I give this to God I give the owing of any debt from this person to God. I will hold my peace and let the Lord fight my battles. I don't want anything bad to happen to the person who hurt me. I release them from any debt that I feel like they owe me. I will not let anger, bitterness, frustration, or any negative emotion take root in and live in my heart. Today, I choose to forgive.

Let me say this to you: As you forgive, guard your heart. You can't keep opening yourself up to people who don't know how to treat you. Some people don't have the things of God in mind for you. Some have been sent on assignment from the devil to get close enough to you to hurt you. You must discern why people are trying to connect with you. Discern whether they come in peace. What are their intentions? What are their motives? You will know them by their fruit. You will know them by the way they treat you on a regular basis. You will know them by the emotions they bring out of you.

There are some people who are repeat offenders. They constantly bring you to tears. They constantly make you angry, scared, bitter, or leave you emotionally bleeding. That's when you have to be bold enough to call a spade a spade and admit to yourself, this person does not even like me. This person is a hater. This person is not good for me to have in my life. Loving and being connected to this person is hurting me.

Sometimes you're entertaining haters and/or hurters. You must recognize who they are and make the decision to cut the drama and end the negative, harmful, and sometimes abusive cycles. Be discerning. Is that a Saul in your life? You helped them in their time of need and now they're jealous of you and stabbing you in the back? Is that a Peninnah in your life? Trying to say that they're your friend? Trying to say that she's a sister but she's really angry at you because you have so much favor in your life?

We're in the days when someone can call you friend, or sister, or brother and not like you at all. In actuality they're jealous or vengeful. Don't let this reality make you walk around paranoid. Everyone is not a hater, jealous, or vengeful. Let's not get spooky and scary with this, but keep your ears and eyes open and discern where people are coming from. Then deal with people accordingly.

Forgiveness does not mean you continue in relationship with everyone who hurts you, especially if it's not your spouse (who is not abusive), your parent, your child, or one of your siblings. I personally fight for these relationships. But outside of these close family relationships, you may have to cut some people out of your life. If they have to go, they have to go.

Some people cannot go where God is taking you when He is shifting you to your "next." Naomi had to leave Orpah behind, but Ruth held on to her. Ruth was committed to Naomi and therefore she was able to share in the blessings that God had in store for Naomi. Ruth was blessed through her connection to Naomi. But guess what? Naomi was also blessed by her connection to Ruth because Ruth wanted to be a blessing to her as well. They were in covenant, and in covenant relationships both parties are blessed. Not just one.

It truly does matter who you are connected to and who you allow to be connected to you! Make sure that you form and nurture kingdom relationships that are mutually beneficial.

When people who are in your life for the wrong reasons bring forth negative emotions, consider if you need to let them go. When people in your life hurt you, including those that truly love and honor you, don't let the negative emotions take root in your heart. Forgive quickly. Communicate your feelings about the situation, come to a place of conflict resolution, decide how you will move forward with the relationship or your connection to that person, and let go of the hurt, the anger, the frustration, and any bitterness. Don't hold on to it. Let it go!

CHAPTER 7

FROM BITTER TO BLESSED

When Naomi came back to Bethlehem, she was bitter, but she ended up blessed. She was blessed by God through her covenant connection with her daughter-in-law Ruth. When Naomi told Orpah and Ruth that she was leaving Moab, Ruth told her, "Where you go, I'll go."

After Ruth went back to Bethlehem with Naomi, she went to work in Boaz's fields to provide food for herself and Naomi. Naomi was not only Ruth's mother-in-law, but she was also her mentor. Ruth submitted to the mentorship and counsel of Naomi and ended up married to Boaz. They had a son named Obed, who was given to Naomi to raise. Then the testimony of Naomi was that she was no longer bitter, but she was now blessed.

God will send people into your life that will be in your corner. God will give you a posse. God will give you a community or a tribe. God will give you a friend. God will give you a mentor. God will give you a leader. God will give you a mentee, or a spiritual son or daughter. God will give you somebody that will stick to you closer than a sister or a brother, and He will give you someone you can trust that will say to you, "No matter what, I'm with you."

I thank God for the communities and the networks that He has given me to connect with and to build and the people that I lead. We are each other's tribe. We are with each other. We have each other's backs, and we are committed not to hurt each other. That is how we are supposed to relate to each other in the Kingdom of God.

Jesus taught that people will know we belong to Him by our love one for another. We must commit to showing more love to others, especially to those in the community of faith. It's time out for women hating on each other and men competing with one another.

We can put our feet on the devil's neck by constantly making public affirmations of our love and support for each other instead of waging public war against one another. I attended an affirmation service one Saturday. They asked me to come up and speak into the newly affirmed apostle's life. One of the things I said to her as I stood in front of her was, "I'm here for you. You don't have to worry about me gossiping about you by stabbing you in the back. I'm not going to use my words to hurt you. I won't walk in jealousy or envy. I say this publicly. I will always be a supporter. I will always be in your corner."

She received every word with tears in her eyes. I think the tears were because of the unusual public declaration of support. Women have spent so much time beating each other down. This is in general and does not include all women, but some women have a hard time supporting and getting along with other women. It is time for us to rise up and support each other. If you are a woman reading this, I charge you to be committed to not hurting another woman, even if that other woman is hurting you in some way. Put some distance between you, but don't retaliate and definitely don't put a dagger in her back.

You don't have to take an eye for an eye or go tit for tat. Just hold your peace, forgive, distance yourself, and let the Lord fight your battles. The battle really is not yours anyway. The God in you annoys some people, and we already talked about the spirit of jealousy that leads some people to mistreat and dislike or hate on others. People are also dealing with other spirits that won't let them rest when they see others blessed. They have to stir up something to bring drama, division, or discord. They have to start some trouble. Growing up we called them "troublemakers."

For many years, there was a woman who came against my ministry, she came against me in a big way because I brought correction to the way she was dealing with a situation that we were both involved in. Since then, I have learned that people can sing your praises all day long, but if you really want to know how people feel about you, correct or rebuke them. If they are not really for you or committed to you, the truth shall come out! This sister in Christ turned on me and became my enemy. She spread some negative and false information amongst other women who once supported me and my ministry. She slandered my name and came against my reputation. I was hurt, but I continued walking in love. I did not retaliate. and to this day I still would not call her name and expose her for what she did to me. People will never know who she is unless they are one of the ones she talked about me to. I never prayed against her. I never said, "God get her."

As a matter of fact, I prayed for her. She cost me money because my books weren't selling, doors were closing, I was no longer being invited to come to preach at churches that were under her influence. People that once supported me were no longer supporting me. And doors of opportunity were closed that once were open. I no longer had favor in places where I used to have favor. I walked through a very dry and barren season that lasted years because of the lies and rumors that were spread about me.

God gave this woman so many chances to repent, but she didn't, and God dealt with her. It broke my heart. It grieved my heart because I love God's people, and I never want to see anyone have to hurt or suffer consequences because of their actions against me that they will not repent of. My prayer for people who mistreat me is, "God have mercy."

That's the prayer that we have to pray for our enemies or those who come against us. "Lord, have mercy!" because guess what? God will deal with your enemies. You have to pray for God to have mercy on those who try to intentionally harm or destroy you. We are to pray for our enemies.

Extending mercy through forgiveness is an act of obedience. God blesses those who obey Him. There is a blessing coming to you when you deal mercifully with others and when you allow the nature and character of God to exude out of you. God is pleased when you forgive others no matter how much they don't deserve it.

I'll never forget the first time I was told I had to forgive the people who had hurt me. My response was, I'm not forgiving them. You don't know what they did to me. Look how they are treating me! They don't deserve to be forgiven!"

God's response to me was, "I know they don't deserve to be forgiven, but you must forgive in order for you to be free from the emotional turmoil that you are holding on to. Forgive them and the anger and pain will eventually go away. If you do not forgive them, the anger and pain will stay. You will be tied to your offender."

That was almost enough to make me forgive. Then God said this, "You did not deserve to be forgiven either, but I forgave you for all the dirty, nasty things that you have done. Are you greater than me?"

That humbled me, and I forgave. Since then, I have forgiven so many people. Some I had to stop being in friendship or relationship with. Others are still in my life. As I said in an earlier chapter, you have to forgive and discern the best way to move forward with the ones you forgive. Do they stay or do you let them go? I chose to end the relationship with this woman, but I did forgive her.

I could have been like Naomi and become bitter over this situation to the extent where I would get depressed or maybe even give up on my ministry and my destiny. But I did not get bitter. I was deeply hurt. I won't lie to you about that. Forgiving her was a process. It took me forgiving her over and over again every time the pain of betrayal hit my heart. Many nights I prayed for

God to take away the pain. It took lots of praying and getting deeper into the Word of God. It took me holding on to God's unchanging hand like never before, but I made it! I came out of a bitter situation. I'm still going strong with my mandate. I have received many accolades and promotions. I can write this today and say that like Naomi, God has taken me from bitter to blessed.

Obedience to God's command to love and forgive made the difference when it came to my blessing of emotional healing. God blesses obedience. Let me say it again. There is a blessing coming to you when you obey God. This applies not just in the area of showing mercy and forgiving others, but it applies to every area of your daily walk with God.

It's time to obey God and walk into your blessings. Stop going down the wrong path when God has told you not to go down that path anymore. Stop dealing with people that God has told you to cut off. Stop being in relationships that you know are not of God. Make up your mind to get to a position where you ae in a posture to just obey God. Strive to obey God in everything. Not in some things, but in all things. Sometimes, we want to pick and choose what we obey when it comes to directives from God. You cannot be too blessed and highly favored to be stressed if you're in disobedience.

Ruth told Naomi, "I'm going with you."

She knew Naomi was a blessed woman. She knew that Naomi had something she needed. And not only was Naomi too blessed and highly favored to be stressed, but Ruth also became too blessed and highly favored to be stressed because she took care of Naomi. She went out and worked in the fields and brought food home for Naomi. She provided for Naomi, and Naomi gave her wisdom. Naomi told her how to get a husband. Naomi said, "Boaz has paid some attention to you. You have favor with him. You go down to that field, and you lay at his feet. Uncover his feet. And when he wakes up and sees you, tell him you want him to be your kinsman redeemer." (She didn't say this literally. I'm paraphrasing.)

That's the closest thing to a proposal that I see a woman making to a man in the Bible, but that's another book for another day.

Naomi told Ruth to tell Boaz she wanted him to be her kinsman redeemer. Ruth did what Naomis said, and she got her husband. Naomi told her to get real pretty smelling, look real pretty. And go down there and get your man, and she did just that and she got her man.

As a result of how Ruth treated Naomi, she received the blessing of marrying Boaz and giving birth to Obed. Naomi received the blessing of being able to nurture and raise Obed as her own son. Obed was the grandfather of David, and as you know, Jesus came through the lineage of David. This is an example of divine covenant for advancing the Kingdom of God. Let me say it again. It really does matter who you are connected to. God-ordained relationships must be established to advance God's Kingdom in the earth realm!

Through covenant relationships, God will allow you to be blessed by what somebody else gives birth to. God will allow you to take part in building up and nurturing the vision that He puts in another person's belly. God will use what's in other people and how He blesses other people to bless you! And He will use what He has put inside of you to be a blessing to others.

Just as there is a Kingdom purpose in connections, there is also a personal blessing in having the right connections. Just as Ruth was blessed by her connection to Naomi and her words of wisdom, Naomi received a blessing through what Ruth carried in her belly. She was able to hold the blessing that Ruth gave birth to, through her obedience to her words of counsel, to her own bosom. She was able to hold her manifested blessing and receive her joy back!

God will bring you from a place of feeling bitter to feeling blessed. During every breaking season, there comes a time of breakthrough. God will allow you to hold your blessing so close to you that you can feel your heart beating with joy. You will be able to feel the peace and the tenderness of broken pieces being put back together again. You will feel yourself begin to breathe again as the bitterness melts away, and you will be able to stand up and say, "Don't call me bitter. Call me blessed. For God has blessed me. God has taken me from bitter to blessed!

CHAPTER 8

GOD'S POWER OVER STRESS

Naomi's life was no longer bitter. God turned things around for her. God is no respecter of persons. Your breakthrough may not have come yet. You may still be in the middle of a stressful situation. Let me say this to you, God is working in the middle of that situation for your good. God is still working in the middle of every situation for the good of those who love Him and are called by His name for His purpose.

Don't worry. Don't get stressed out. If you are going through a rough season, things will turn around for you. Weeping and distress may last for a time, but there is a time when your joy will be restored. God will take away the bitterness. He will heal you from the brokenness. God will remove the pain. He will bring you from a bitter place into your blessed place. Just hold on while God works things out and turns things around for you.

While you're waiting, God will give you wisdom. You will develop more patience, and your faith will increase. Things may get a little rocky sometimes, but in your due season, you will come to a point of stability.

I talked about that ride and argument that I had in the car with my husband. Throughout the years, God has brought us both to a place of stability in our emotions and the way we engage each other in disagreements. This stability allows us to agree to disagree, and even when we disagree, we can disagree in a way that we do not deeply wound each other. There are certain words we don't say to each other, and we make every effort to end the conflict quickly and come to a healthy resolution.

I thank God for this growth and wisdom. As a woman, I used to be so emotionally sensitive, but now there are things that used to hurt me deeply that no longer have the same impact. There is a certain level of maturity that you can get to where you are shielded from the arrows aimed at your heart, intentionally or unintentionally, because sometimes when we are not healed, we take everything personal and get easily offended. When you are healed from past hurts and get to a certain level of emotional maturity, what used to hurt you and devastate you emotionally is not going to be able to hurt you so deeply any longer.

You may have to deal with some surface wounds, but for the most part, it's going to be like arrows bouncing off of your shield of faith and breastplate of righteousness.

Trust God to give you an inner healing where He takes away the sting of the frustration and the pain. If you are still hurting from pain of your past, ask God to heal you. Go to God like the woman with the issue of blood and touch the hem of His garment in prayer. Be like Naomi, who although she was hurting and bitter, got up and went back to where she knew God was. Do whatever you have to do to get into the presence of God. God will heal you. He will restore your joy, your hope, and your faith. He will connect you to people who will be a blessing to you as you are a blessing to them.

I wrote this book on assignment to let you know that you are too blessed and highly favored to be stressed. Even though the stress may come or it might be present right now, as you continue to walk this thing out, as you continue to go through the process, as you continue to let God deal with the pain, as you continue to let the trials and tribulations nurture and birth out patience, then you'll be able to make it through every storm.

You will be able to walk through every storm, every trial, and every struggle knowing that God is bringing you from the trial to triumph. You'll be able to walk through life knowing that you have gone from being a victim to being victorious. Your victory is already written. It's a done deal. God's not going to allow the enemy to get the best of you. He's not going to allow circumstances to get the best of you. He's not going to allow sickness to get the best of you. He's not going to allow loneliness to get the best of you. He's not going to allow the devil to get the best of you. There is a promise over your life for victory. God will take care of you. He will situate you in a place and position around people where you will be provided for, where you will be protected, a place where you will be taken care of and blessed.

That's what God has taught me in my life. Many times, things would be going great, and I would be skipping along as happy as I can be. Then the enemy came in and tried to spoil it. Any time things are going beautifully and you're on a high and feeling great, don't be surprised if the devil shows up. The Bible lets you know to stay alert because, the devil, your adversary is prowling around seeking whom he can devour. And he will use what and who he can use to try to knock you down. But keep your warrior stance and always have it in your heart that God's got you, the enemy is defeated, your blessings are coming, and stress is leaving.

No matter what, have faith in God for His best when it comes to your life. The time will come when you walk into the manifested promises that God has over your life. The Bible declares that your eyes have not seen, nor have your ears heard, neither has it entered into your heart the things that God has in store for you. I dare you to declare that over your life and believe and receive it!

I'm not living in LaLa Land. I know things have been hard for you at times. I know people have disappointed you and some have walked away from you. I know it hurts. But guess what? God is with you through it all and He is working on your behalf. When things get difficult to handle, know that things will not always be so hard. Seasons come and seasons go. Your season of things getting easier is coming around again. God is going to bring a blessing to you.

God is going to give you better. God is going to bring people into your life that are going to treat you better. He is going to bring people into your life that know your value. God is going to bring people into your life that know how to treat you. God's going to bring people into your life that love and appreciate you for who you are. They're going to honor and respect you. They will be a blessing to you.

Yes, warfare is real, and I truly believe that the magnitude of the warfare in your life shows you the magnitude of the blessing that God has for you, as well as the assignment, mandate, and mantle or anointing that's on your life. Great warfare has been coming against the plan of God for your life! Great pain has been coming against a greater promise. You may have gotten a bad report that is coming against great victory. Don't worry. Don't stress out. No weapon formed against you shall prosper!

Nothing can stop the Word, plan, and hand of God over your life. There's nothing too hard for God. There's nothing too big for God. There's nothing that God cannot handle. There's nothing that God will allow to come into your life that He has not given you the ability to handle and conquer. God's grace is sufficient for you. You're going to make it through every storm. You're going to make it through every rough season. You're going to make it over every mountain of trouble, trials, and tribulation that stands in front of you.

Jesus told the disciples that He was giving them keys to the Kingdom of heaven that they could use to bind and loose, which means to not allow (bind)and allow (loose). He told them that whatever they allowed on earth would be allowed in heaven and whatever they disallowed on earth would be disallowed in heaven. He also told them how to conquer the mountain. He told them that if they believed and did not doubt, they could speak to the mountain and tell it to move and be cast into the sea and it will be done. You can move the mountain, but you have to use your faith and your keys.

Recently, my husband woke me up about 5:00 in the morning, saying, "Did you see my keys? I can't find my keys."

He had lost his keys, As I recall that incident, I see God restoring the keys. God is giving you back your keys. It's time to use the keys of your authority! Jesus has given us the keys of the Kingdom. He has given us the authority to bind and loose, which means we can either disallow or allow some things in the earth realm. But just as my husband had lost the ability to use his physical keys to our house because he could not find them, you may have lost the faith to use your spiritual keys of your authority pertaining to the Kingdom of God. You must hold on to your faith and use your keys. If your faith in the ability to use your keys is lost, you cannot use them. I see God restoring to you the use of your keys.

My husband's keys were not really lost. He had just misplaced them and forgotten where he put them. Sometimes it's not that we have lost our keys or even that we have lost the faith to use our keys. Sometimes it's just that we forget that we have them and that we have been given permission and authority to use them.

God has given you keys of power and authority. He has given you the keys of the Kingdom. The keys of the Kingdom are in your faith and in your vocal cords. God has given you the ability to open your mouth and speak over your life. He has given you the ability to bind and to loose. God has given you the ability to speak some things into the earth realm. I know the church doesn't believe that anymore. We have gotten so earthly bound that we are not making a heavenly impact!

Jesus told the disciples that when they used their Kingdom keys, Heaven would back them up. In the same way, when you use your Kingdom keys, Heaven will back you up! Whatever you allow or do not allow on earth, as you speak it, God will back you up!

It's time to use your keys. It's time to tap into the supernatural realm. It's time to open your mouth and declare a thing. Open your mouth and speak your own breakthrough in the name of Jesus. Open your mouth and speak healing over your own life. Speak over your own marriage. Speak over your finances. Speak over your bank account. Speak over that next assignment. Speak over that next job. Speak over that promotion.

Speak restoration, peace, and unity over that marriage. Speak over that husband. Speak over those children. Use your keys.

Life and circumstances have put you on mute. It's time to come off mute. Maybe you have lost the faith to use your keys. It's time to get your faith back. You only need the faith of a mustard seed to speak to that mountain that's trying to cause you stress. As you believe and do not doubt, the mountain will be removed by the power of God. Don't let it stress you out. You've prayed about it. Now let your words line up with the Word of God and say something about it. If it's in your way, tell that mountain, it's got to move!
If it's causing you stress, tell that mountain to move!

Let me say this one last thing as I close out this chapter. Sometimes stress comes as a result of having too much to do on your plate. I challenge you to not put another thing on your plate until you clear some things off. Operate in the Omega anointing (the power of God to finish) and complete some of the tasks that you need to complete so you can make room for what's coming next.

Taking things off of your plate also means having the courage and the wisdom to say no. Before you say yes to more to do, pray and ask God if it is a God assignment. It may be a good assignment, but you must preserve your oil primarily for your mandated assignments. Pray and don't move until you get that yes in your spirit. If you do not get a yes, just say no.

It's important to put this in place, because sometimes you get stressed out because you are tired. You're tired because you have too much on your plate. It's time to clean and balance your plate. On our dinner plates, we're supposed to have space between the vegetables, the meat, and the carbs. We are supposed to have less carbs, more vegetables and about six ounces of meat (if you eat meat. Some substitute another form of protein for meat). The point I'm making is there is supposed to be space between everything on your dinner plate The same applies to your plate of things to do in your day-to-day schedule. There is supposed to be space on the plate. Your schedule is not supposed to be so full that you're burning out or stressed out. Operate in God's power that has been given to you to finish assignments and structure your life. You can do it. You can do all things through Christ who gives you the ability and the power.

Remember that you have been given power and authority by God. Remember that greater is God living in you than any power in this world. Remember, that even when you cannot find the strength or the faith to use the power or the keys given to you, that the power of God is backing you up. After you have done all you can do, just stand in the power of His might. God's power is always working things out for your good. When life tries to overwhelm you, slip into the secret place with Him. God will give you a peace that surpasses all understanding. God's power will bring you through every valley and over every mountain when the circumstances, issues, challenges, and struggles of life try to get the best of you.

No weapon formed against you will succeed.
Isaiah 54:17 (NLT)

Be strong in the Lord and in his mighty power.
Put on all of God's armor so that you will be able
to stand firm against all strategies of the devil.
Ephesians 6:10 (NLT)

Yet in all these things, we are more than
conquerors (and gain an overwhelming victory)
through Christ who loved us (so much that He
died for us.)
Romans 8:37 (Amplified Version)

CHAPTER 9

BLESSINGS, PRAYER, AND PROPHETIC DECLARATION

I speak the blessings of the LORD over your life as I close out this book with prayer and prophetic declaration.

Lord, I thank you that the person reading this is too blessed and highly favored to be stressed. Thank you for making them a royal priesthood. Thank you for making them wonderfully and fearfully made. They are blessed to be called your son or your daughter.

I pray for the person reading this book that might be feeling a little stressed out, bitter or discouraged. I pray that you will give them your peace that surpasses all understanding. I pray that you will seal your word upon their heart that you are with them and that you will never leave or forsake them. Let them know and believe that you are working things out for their good. I pray for that person that has a bad diagnosis or prognosis. I speak healing over their life, and I pray that they will know in their heart that you are still a healer. I speak over the one that's believing to buy a house, believing for their spouse, believing for their children, believing for a promotion on the job, believing for a new job, or believing for the money to pay their bills. I speak over that person that's believing for their ministry, believing to be able to finish that book, or believing to birth that business. I speak breakthroughs and blessings over them now. I speak over that person that's believing for a successful, God-filled, Spirit-led relationship, I pray that you give them all the answers to their prayers and the desires of their heart as they delight themselves in you.

I pray for the person that still has unforgiveness or bitterness in their heart, that they will let it go. I pray for the person that's burdened, heavy laden, and weary. I pray that as they come to you in prayer, that you will give them rest. I pray that you anoint the one reading this right now with fresh oil. Pour fresh anointing oil on them now LORD. Pour the oil like Samuel poured oil on David's head. Anoint them for the mandate and the measure that you have assigned to them. Anoint them afresh and anew.

Thank you for the fresh oil of the anointing being poured out. LORD, let there be no distractions that will take them off the path that you have ordained for them. Help them to stay focused. I pray that they will keep their hands to the plow and do the assignment and do it with the Omega anointing oil. Activate the Omega anointing that is on the inside of them. Activate the Omega anointing in their belly Lord. Activate the anointing to finish the mandate, to take their mountain, and operate in their measure without being bitter, burnt out, or stressed out.

Help them to look at their plates and see what needs to be taken off. Guide them as they look at their plates and make sure there is space on the plate for them to take time to spend time with you, for them to take time to spend with their family and loved ones, that they would be able to spend time on their hobbies, spend time nurturing and taking care of their bodies and their health. Let them practice self-love by taking time to rest, eat a healthy diet, and exercise. Help them to take time to enjoy life more abundantly and to stop and smell the roses.

Thank you, Lord. I praise you. I worship you, Lord, and I magnify your name.

I pray that they have no more wrong connections or relationships – platonic or romantic leading to marriage. Thank you for the plan that you have for putting the right people in their life. Thank you for the blessings you have in store for them. I thank you that what you have for them is for them and no one can stop it. I thank you that they are truly too blessed and highly favored to be stressed. In Jesus name I pray. Amen.

Prophetic Declaration For Your Life

I prophetically declare that you are blessed and highly favored by the LORD. I declare that the plan of God shall manifest in your life as you continue to walk with Him. I declare that you are not a victim of your circumstances, but you are victorious. I declare that no weapon formed against you will prosper. I declare that you shall prosper and be in good health even as your soul prospers. I declare that by the stripes of Jesus Christ you are healed physically, emotionally, and spiritually, I declare that you are blessed. Your children are blessed. Your household is blessed. Your bank account is blessed. I declare that you are anointed for your mandate. I declare that you are anointed for your assignment on the mountain of the sphere of influence that God has for you to operate in. You are anointed to take care of those children. You are anointed for breakthrough. You are anointed for victory! I declare that as you meditate on God's Word day and night, you shall make your way prosperous and have good success. I declare that as you delight in the Lord and His Word, everything you touch shall prosper. I declare and decree that you are too blessed and highly favored by the Lord to be stressed!

Amen and praise God!

ABOUT THE AUTHOR

Rebecca Simmons is a woman after God's own heart. More than anything, she loves God and is grateful for His faithfulness towards her. She is the author of 15 books. She is a prolific writer and speaker and preacher with a goal to positively impact and change the lives of those who read her books and listen to her speak and preach. She is an intercessory prayer warrior and an affirmed apostolic leader who keeps her ears open to hear the voice and Words of God. She is passionate about her call to preach, prophesy, write, publish, and teach the doctrine of the Kingdom of Heaven. She is a powerful speaker with a testimony that God is using for His glory. She ministers deliverance through the power of the Holy Spirit and is courageous when it comes to spiritual warfare. She is a virtuous woman who has seen God work wondrously in her life.

For the past, 20 years, she has served as Pastor of New Creation Christian Ministries working side by side with Pastor Anthony Simmons, her husband of over 29 years. They have four children, four grandchildren, a great grandson, and many spiritual sons and daughters whom they love, cover spiritually, and mentor.

She is the owner operator of Diligence Publishing Company since 2003, where she diligently endeavors to help other authors to publish and release the Kingdom books that God has mandated for them to birth out.

Rebecca Simmons is the author of *Nobody's Business, The Cry of A Woman's Heart, Daddy Love, Don't Die In The Wilderness, Pump Up The Power, Making Marriage And Relationships Work, Man Problems, Moving Forward When Life Lets You Down, You're Better Than That: Real Talk for Ladies Who Want God's Best, God Is A Promise Keeper, Manifesting Kingdom: Unlocking God's Blessings and Abundance In Your Life, Your Book Matters: How To Successfully Write and Publish Your Book, Kayla's Day, Greatness Inside* and this, her latest work, *Too Blessed and Highly Favored To Be Stressed..* Most of her books are available on Amazon.com, her websites, and wherever books are sold.

She is the Founder of Woman To Woman Empowerment Group on Facebook, Women Destined For Victory Alliance and Academy and Manifesting Kingdom Global Network (MKGN)

Her websites are www.manifestingkingdom.com, www.nccmonline.org, www.womendestinedforvictory.com and www.dpc-books.com. You can connect with her on Facebook @ pastorrebeccasimmons or by email at rebeccasimmonsministries@gmail.com.

ORDER INFORMATION

You can order additional copies of Too Blessed and Highly Favored To Be Stressed by emailing the author directly using the email address below.

Dr. Rebecca Simmons

rebeccasimmonsministries@gmail.com

Books are available at Amazon.com, BN.com Kindle and Your Local Bookstores (By Request)

Please leave a review for this book on Amazon and let other readers know how much you enjoyed reading it.

Thank you!

www.ingramcontent.com/pod-product-compliance
Lightning Source LLC
Chambersburg PA
CBHW052218090426
42741CB00010B/2585

* 9 7 9 8 9 8 6 9 1 7 3 6 8 *